Robert 'Troublechurch' Browne of Tolethorpe and the Separatist Movement

by

The Pupils of
Ryhall CE Primary School, Rutland,
and John Haden

First published by Barny Books,
All rights reserved
Copyright © John Haden 2013

ISBN No: 978.1.906542.61.0
Publishers: Barny Books, 76 Cotgrave Lane, Tollerton,
              Nottingham. NG12 4FY
              Tel: 0115 937 5147
              www.barnybooks.co.uk

Copies of this book may be obtained from:

ARIES Project   and   Ryhall CofE Primary
School
13 St Albans Close,   Church Street, Ryhall,
OAKHAM, Rutland   STAMFORD, Lincs.
LE15 6EW   PE9 4HR
Tel: +44(0)1572 70428   Tel: +44(0)1780 762447

Contents

1. Introduction: Who was Robert Browne?

About three hundred and eighty years ago, a very old and very stout man was taken from Achurch, a small village in the Nene valley not far from Oundle, to Northampton Gaol. He was too old and too fat to ride a horse so they put him on a feather bed on a cart and took him about twenty miles off to prison. He had assaulted the village constable during an argument over the non-payment of a tax. The old man did not last long in prison. In the register of burials of St Giles Church in Northampton, the parish priest recorded in 1633: *'Mr Browne, Parson of Achurch, was buryed the viiith of October.'*

This short book is an account of the family background, the life and the work of that 'Mr Browne'. The few accounts in print of his life tell us that he was one of the Brownes of Stamford, the leading family of that fine town. He was also the man who started a Separatist movement in the Elizabethan Church of England. They became known as the 'Brownists' and from this, he was given the nick-name, 'Troublechurch'. A very small group of these Separatist believers became much better known when they decided to leave England in the early 17th Century, going first to Holland and then, in 1620, across the Atlantic Ocean. They became known as the Pilgrim Fathers and some say that they were the founders of the United States of America.

The true story of 'Mr Browne, Parson of Achurch' deserves to be better known. We set out to find all that is known about the family from which he came, the place where he was born and the story of his life. We began by asking questions:

1. Why is Stamford in Lincolnshire such an attractive town with so many fine churches and other buildings?

2. Do we have to go to Church?

3. What was Tolethorpe like when Robert Browne was born there about 1550?

4. How did Browne become a 'trouble' to the Church of England in the time of Queen Elizabeth I?

5. How do we look after the very old in our families and our communities?

6. What happened to Browne's followers?

This book is the tenth in the American Roots in English Soil (ARIES) Project series. In each book, pupils from schools and communities in Eastern England have worked with John Haden to publish short accounts of the stories of individuals from their own areas who went on to play a part in the founding and development of English Speaking America. They are books written with schools, rather than for schools, to be read by visitors to the places we have written about, churches, grand and modest houses, villages and towns. We hope also that they will be of interest to the communities which they describe.

2. The Brownes of Stamford

Celia Fiennes wrote in 1697 that Stamford in Lincolnshire *'is as fine a town built of stone as may be seen'*. She was the grand-daughter of a Lord and an ancestor of Sir Ranulph Fiennes, an intrepid lady who wrote a book about her travels into every corner of England. Stamford today still has a wonderful set of medieval church buildings and the best set of Georgian town houses in England. From the Meadows down by the River Welland, the panorama of the town is still, in the words of Richard K. and Ben D. of Ryhall CE Primary *'breathtaking, amazing, rich and beautiful; you can see six churches from the Meadows.'* If you visit the town and are looking for somewhere to eat, they also recommend *'the Cosy Club in Horseshoe Lane for its spectacular food.'*

Stamford's beautiful streets have been used as a film set for *'Pride and Prejudice' (2005)* and *'The Da Vinci Code' (2006)* and for the BBC TV production of *'Middlemarch' (1994)*, all of which begs the question: 'Why is Stamford such an attractive town?' How was it possible for the people of a relatively small market town in a very rural area to build in such fine style for centuries?

The simple answer is 'both stone and sheep'. 'Stone' because Stamford is surrounded by supplies of excellent honey-coloured limestone. 'Barnack Rag' was quarried to the south. 'Stamford Freestone' was found even nearer the town and at Casterton. The Romans used stone from the quarries of Clipsham and Ancaster, and Ketton limestone has been used since Tudor times. These quarries supplied the stone for cathedrals, castles, colleges and country houses all over Eastern England and provided Stamford with superb building materials. The village of Collyweston, just to the south-west, is famous for limestone slates, stone which can be split to form the beautiful roofs on many Stamford houses.

But you still need to be rich to build in stone. Much of the wealth of Stamford came from sheep and the value of the wool they carry on their backs. Even today, the Speaker of the House of Lords sits on a 'woolsack'. In Parliament, at the heart of our Government, this 'woolsack' has been used since the 14th Century to remind us that one of the foundations of England's early prosperity was the wool trade.

Lincoln Longwool sheep by Isabel A.

Lincoln Longwool sheep were developed over the centuries to produce a heavy fleece of strong wool for making cloth. They are a calm breed so that makes them very easy to handle. These sheep are the largest of the Longwool sheep family in Britain. In the old days, the sheep were walked from the farms to Stamford Sheep Market to be sold and slaughtered to provide mutton for the butchers' shops, grease for soap and tallow for candles. Great numbers of Lincoln Longwool sheep were exported to many countries to improve the size and wool quality of their native breeds. Today, people still keep small flocks of Lincoln Longwools as a rare breed.

(by Evie H. and Isabel A.)

Eating places in The Sheep Market, Stamford

Stamford still has a part of the town called 'the Sheep Market' and there is a very old pub nearby called the Golden Fleece, celebrating the value of wool. Just up the road in St Paul's Street, there is another very old pub which was called the Woolpack until the new owners renamed it the Tobie Norris.

At least eight generations of Browne are recorded in Stamford before Robert Browne of Tolethorpe, and most of them had a connection with the wool trade. Some of them had links with the French port of Calais, where the Cross-

Channel ferries still dock. Seven hundred years ago, in the early years of the 14th Century, England was at war with France. Edward III, King of England, won a great battle at Crecy in Northern France and nearby Calais was captured by the English. Before that, English wool had been sold to European merchants in markets such as Stamford and then taken into Europe through the Belgian cities of Antwerp and Bruges. But after 1347, Edward III encouraged English merchants to settle in Calais.

The name Staple was given to the trade of export of wool first used in 1314 and still in use today. The Staple was also the group of twenty six English merchants who were incorporated as the Company of the Staple at Calais. They were the merchants who managed the wool trade. William Browne was elected to be a member of the Staple. He bought wool from farmers and sent it to Calais to be sold there.

(by Richard K. and Corey R.)

The port, now in English hands, became the trading centre for English wool on the other side of the English Channel. For centuries, if you had a flock of sheep anywhere in England and wanted the best price for your wool, you sold it to a merchant who would pack it into a woolsack and send it to Calais, where merchants from all over Europe could bid for the best wool they could buy.

Every sack of wool had a 'mark' showing whose it was. The Brownes used a heart shape with a B and a cross at the top. It was their 'merchants' mark', a bit like the trademarks used today by companies like McDonalds and Tesco.

(by Richard K. and Corey R.)

The merchant mark used by the Brownes by Keiran L.

Having just one port for the selling of English wool into Europe made it easier for the King to tax the wool trade. The arrangement made a lot of money, for the King from these taxes and for the merchants or 'Staplers' from the profits on the sale of wool. They had a headquarters in the City of London at 'Staple Inn', a fine half-timbered building which still stands on High Holborn. They were one of the first of many City Companies, each enjoying a monopoly of one trade such as the Grocers, the Fishmongers and the Butchers. These Companies still exist in the City of London and some of them still have their old Halls where they met to discuss business and to dine together.

The coat of arms of the Staple of Calais had a lion at the top to represent the country of England. We still have three lions on the badge which the England football team wear. Underneath, the waves symbolise the English Channel, so the arms show 'England over the Channel'.
(by Richard K. and Corey R.)

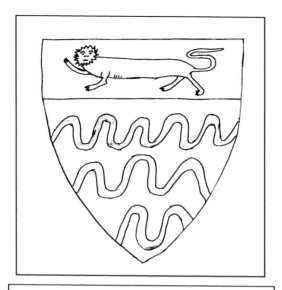

The coat of arms of the Staple of Calais by
Joshua S.

Today, we use the word 'staple' in two senses, as the main food which people eat as in 'a staple diet of bread or rice', and as a small metal wire for holding papers, as in 'stapled together'. But it is also still used by wool experts to describe the length of the fibres in a sample of wool, as in 'short staple', suitable for making tough things like carpets, and 'long staple', much higher quality, useful for spinning and weaving and making clothes to wear.

In the Middle Ages, some of the best wool in Europe came from England and Wales, and especially from the Lincolnshire Wolds and the Cotswolds in the west. St Peter's Abbey in Gloucester had flocks of over ten thousand sheep by 1300 and across England there were thought to be up to eighteen million sheep sheared every year. All this wool commanded very high prices and in the 13th and 14th

Centuries many towns and even villages in Eastern England became rich enough to rebuild their parish church. This produced a whole new flowering of English architecture. The great 'wool churches' at Salle and Cawston in Norfolk, and at Fairford and Chipping Campden in the Cotswolds are like huge Gothic greenhouses dominating tiny villages in a wide-open landscape. Their style is called Perpendicular because that is what it is, soaring walls and spires of stone pointing to the sky.

Of all the English Counties, Lincolnshire still has the most medieval churches, many of them built or rebuilt from the profits of the wool trade. When the merchants of Boston started to build the tower of their parish church, the famous Boston Stump, their town was the biggest wool port in England so they built the tallest parish church tower. In Grantham, the tower of the parish church carries what many believe is the finest steeple in England. Only the spire of Salisbury Cathedral is higher. When the people of Louth built the Perpendicular spire of their parish church, said to be the most perfect in England, they placed small stone heads of sheep at the four corners of the star-burst vault under the tower, because sheep had made it possible for a small market town to create such a thing of beauty. In all these towns, just one parish church served the community but in Stamford no less then thirteen parish churches jostled
for space in a town of only a few thousand people.

When the members of the Staple of Calais elected William Browne of Stamford to be a member, the Brownes had been trading in cloth and wool in Stamford for four generations. They were 'drapers' with a shop and a wool-hall in the town and they had served in many important local roles, particularly as 'Alderman' or Mayor of the town. But to become a 'Stapler' meant something much greater.

William was now an overseas trader with a share in the rich pickings of the Staplers' monopoly over English wool exports.

His brother, John, was also his business partner and would soon himself be elected to the Staple. Their sister, Alice, married into a Coventry family involved in wool trading from the Midlands and the Cotswold. Later, William's daughter, Elizabeth, married another Calais Stapler, based in Oxfordshire with connections in the wool-exporting port of Southampton. The Browne brothers were building a strong business network based on close family connections, and with strong links with the ports of Boston, Lynn, Ipswich, London and Southampton. They were making good money by sending woolsacks with the Browne merchants' mark through Calais into Europe.

William and John Browne would have bought wool from producers throughout Lincolnshire, from Yorkshire to the north and across to the Chilterns and the Cotswolds in the west. The wool would be brought by packhorses and mules to their wool hall in Stamford where it would be graded and weighed. It would be packed into sacks and sent down the River Welland or the River Nene to the East Coast ports of Boston, Lynn and Ipswich or across country and down to Southampton.

With English ships facing French and other pirates in the Channel, the merchants would spread their stock of wool across many vessels to reduce the risk and ensure that the ships sailed in convoy for the short voyage to Calais. Once safely there, their wool would be marketed to the many merchants from France and Germany, Belgium and Italy keen to buy the best English wool for their cloth-makers.

In spite of all the troubles of England in the 15th Century, the Wars of the Roses, the appalling weather and outbreaks of the Plague, the Browne brothers of Stamford steadily built up their wealth and they made their money work for them. Along with the other Staplers, they regularly lent money to the King, (whichever King was on the throne of England at the time). They provided other merchants with loans and mortgages and, in spite of the complicated calculations of exchange rates with merchants from Europe, they developed their business empire.

Just as today, rich men make money from property, so the Brownes used their wealth from wool to build up their holdings of land and buildings, shops and land within the town of Stamford and manors and farms in the surrounding area. Some they tenanted out to earn rent. Others they held as security against loans and when the recipient of the loan could not repay, the Brownes took over the property. As their wool-trading generated cash, they invested more and more in land and buildings until they were probably the largest land-owners in Stamford.

In all this business activity it seems that William, the older brother, was the dominant partner. Just as their father had before them, they both served as Alderman of Stamford, but William's name appears six times on the list, John Browne just three times. In the records of their property, William owned much more than John. When William died in 1489, his will gave two thirds of his property to his wife Margaret and one third to a charity. The property given to the charity amounted to fourteen estates in Lincolnshire outside Stamford, four in Rutland and eight in Northamptonshire together with fifteen properties in Stamford. If this was just one third of his property holding, the total would have been enormous. No wonder he was described by a contemporary recorder as '*a merchant of very wonderful richnesse*', by a long way the richest man in Stamford. Yet he had no direct heir, no son to inherit all his wealth.

Rich men today use their money to support their interests. Very rich men from Russia and from the Middle East buy English football clubs, like Chelsea and Manchester City in the Premier League. The American, Bill Gates, who made a lot of money from his Windows software, has set up a charitable foundation to pour US $25 billion into national and international good causes.

William Browne's world was much smaller. He had traded wool with Europe and probably travelled all over England to buy wool. He had been to Calais and possibly to the cities of Bruges and Antwerp. But his world had limited horizons. No-one had yet been to the Americas, or to most of Africa and the Far East. So William spent his money in his home town, Stamford, and on the church where his father had been buried, All Saints in the Market Place.

All Saints' Church was originally built in 1086 but only a little of the original church remains. It was rebuilt by John and William Browne in the 15ᵗʰ century when the sale of their wool made a lot of money. This paid for the new design of this unique church. They added a hefty roof, a new tower and side chapels too!
(by Eve S., Lucy H. and Leah K.)

The fine new spire which the Browne brothers built for All Saints Church, Stamford in the late 15th century.

Inside All Saints Church, there is more work by the Browne brothers. They demolished the original nave down to the window ledges and then rebuilt it. They added aisles on both the north and south sides and turned them into what are effectively family chapels. Although other changes were added much later, the whole church is still mainly their work today.

Inside All Saints, Stamford, looking east down the nave by Rimini A.

High up in the nave, on the right in Rimini's drawing, the beautiful corbels to support the roof were made of Stamford stone. One corbel was carved as the head of a sheep. He still has a fixated grin on his face! Many other animals were put as corbels too!

(by Eve S., Lucy H. and Leah K.)

18

Sheep head corbel by Owen C.

The church has been a place of worship for over seven hundred years but it is also very much the creation of these two brothers. Their family drapers shop and wool store was right next to the church in Red Lion Square. The Browne merchant mark is still displayed on a stone shield above the chancel arch at the end of the nave. Memorial brasses to them and to their families decorate the aisles, William and Margaret on the South side and John and Margery, and their son Christopher, on the North.

John Browne's family brasses in the North Aisle of All Saints Church, Stamford.

In 2003, the engraved figures from these memorials were used to decorate the two glass doors of the church in memory of William and John Browne, wool merchants of Stamford. William Brown paid for his brass memorial about twenty years before his death. He was obviously a very careful planner!

William Browne's memorial brass from All Saints' Church Stamford.

He is standing on two wool sacks, the source of his wealth. Before William died, he left precise instructions for his burial in the *'chapell of Our Lady on the south side within the church of Alhalowue.....my feete between the water and the wall thereof'*. Buried in the same chapel was his grand-daughter, Margaret Elmes, a child of about eight.

The Browne brothers had achieved their aim of turning the most important of Stamford's parish churches into their family shrine, no doubt helped by the fact that their brother-in-law, Thomas Stokke, was Vicar of All Saints at the time. But for the Brownes, there remained the very important matter of prayer for their souls. At that time, the Church taught that when an individual dies, the soul does not go straight to heaven but into a place or state called purgatory. Even those who died believing in the saving power of Jesus Christ and sure of their eternal salvation still had need of purification by spending time in purgatory before they could enter into the happiness of heaven.

Those of the faithful who were still on earth could help the souls in purgatory by praying for them so it became vitally important to those facing death to have these prayers set up before they died. This teaching led to a whole system of prayers for the dead (*obits* and hence obituary), masses for the dead (*requiems*) and payments of alms to charity in memory of the dead. Rich men could use their money to set up their own arrangements for these and William Browne was rich. He could help the old people of Stamford by setting up an almshouse as a charity to look after them and at the same time he could satisfy his own family's need by insisting that the residents of the almshouse said prayers for their souls every day.

William Browne's Hospital, which is in fact an old people's home, is in Broad Street in Stamford. The Hospital has only ever had twelve people living there, originally ten men and two women. The two women helped all the ten men. Today there is only one man living there and all the other places are occupied by women.

(by Ben D, Ella B, William F and Gabriel O.)

William Browne's Hospital,

The ten men originally lived in cubicles on both sides of the Common Room, a large dormitory in which each man had a window for light. At the end of the Common Room, a carved screen led to a chapel so that even the sick or bed-ridden could hear the services held there. Each of the residents was required to attend the chapel service twice a day, and on Sundays, they had to go to the service at All Saints Church. At all these services, this prayer was said:

'God have mercy upon the souls of William Browne of Stamford and Dame Margaret, his wife and on the soul of Mr Thomas Stokke, founders of this almshouse, and of the souls of their fathers and mothers, and all Christian souls.'

3. Do we have to go to church?

One of the questions we asked in connection with this account of Robert Browne's family background was 'do we have to go to church?' We agreed that the short answer, in 2013, is 'No, we don't have to!' If we want to go to church to worship God, we are free to go but it was very different in the world of William Browne's Stamford, and not just for the twelve old people living in his Hospital. The life of the town revolved around the thirteen parish churches. Everyone was baptised in church, married in church and buried in the churchyard. The great festivals of the Church, the holy days of Christmas, Easter and Pentecost and the feast-days of the saints, punctuated the year. On many of these special days, there were plays and colourful pageants in the streets of the town. Each church had its own guild or charitable fellowship who would take part in these plays but their main role was the support of those in need. If you were rich, you gave money to your guild

At the time William Browne endowed his Hospital, it would have been unthinkable for anyone not to go to church on Sundays and 'holy days'. It was not therefore a particular burden on the ten old men to require them to attend services, although to require them to say specific prayers for the Browne family's souls was an extra duty. Right up to the time of Henry VIII, all these services would have followed the Latin Mass of the Roman Catholic Church, and even when Henry broke with the authority of the Pope by claiming to be the Head of the English Church himself, worship in parish churches continued to be according to the Latin Mass. The old men in the Hospital were called *'bedesmen'* after the beads in the rosary which they would carry when saying their prayers.

William and Margaret Browne had no son but their brother, John, had several. One of these, Christopher, continued in the Browne tradition of public service in Stamford, being elected to the town council of twelve men and becoming Alderman twice. He was a Justice of the Peace in Lincolnshire and in Rutland, and he also had royal connections. His family claimed that he was with the invasion force when Henry Tudor came into Wales from France and established the Tudor dynasty of English Kings as Henry VII. Christopher retained an interest in wool trading and he too was a Stapler of Calais, but he was also a courtier, the first of the family to have a coat of arms and to call himself 'esquire'.

What is said to be Christopher Browne's coat of arms

He decided to move out of the town of Stamford in 1503 to take up the life of a country gentleman, by buying the estate of Tolethorpe Hall, just to the north of the town on the banks of the River Gwash. But he still maintained his links in Stamford and his memorial brass is in the north chapel of All Saints Church, alongside those of his father and grandfather.

Tolethorpe Hall as it was in 1684 from Wright's
'History and Antiquities of Rutland'

From their fine country house, Christopher Browne
and his family would have gone to the services in their parish
church of Little Casterton and followed the Latin Mass. But
as William Browne's nephew, Christopher Browne continued
to be a leading member of the Guild of All Saints Church in
Stamford which his Uncle had founded. They usually met in
the room above the Common Room, the Audit Room, of the
Hospital. But some time after William Browne's death, the
Warden of the Hospital refused to allow the All Saints Guild
to go on meeting in the Audit Room, claiming that this was
reserved for the exclusive use of the Hospital's trustees to
conduct their business. Eventually, the matter came to court
and the Warden lost the dispute. The right of the Guild
members to meet in the very attractive room was re-
established. The links with All Saints Church were
maintained by ensuring that the Vicar of All Saints was one
of the Auditors of the Hospital holding one of the three keys
to the chest in which the records, seals and valuables of

the Hospital charity were held.

Over the centuries, a link developed between the Foundation of Browne's Hospital and the schools in Stamford. In 1871, it was agreed that part of the rich endowments of the Hospital should be used to found a girls school, to be known as Stamford High School and at the same time, funds from the hospital were used for buildings at Stamford School. The badge which William Browne used in honour of his wife, Margaret Stokke, showed a 'stokke' or stork perched on a woolsack with the motto 'jesu me spede' or '+ me spede'. This became the badge of the Stamford Endowed Schools and is still the theme of the Stamford High School for Girls song:

'Give us then that virtue rare,
Courage to do and dare,
Grant us our humble prayer,
Christ me spede'.

The badge of Margaret Stokke which became the
badge of the Stamford Endowed Schools

The next Browne to live at Tolethorpe was Christopher's son Francis. He was the first member of the family to break completely with the family tradition of wool

26

trading as he followed his mother's father into the law. The family made another step up the social ladder when one of Francis Browne's half-brothers married a daughter of the rising family, the Cecils. The Cecils moved to the Burghley estate on the south side of the Welland and it was here that William Cecil built his great house when he became Elizabeth I's Chief Minister. This linked the Browne family to the Cecil's and William   Cecil was a very useful man to know.

Francis Browne died at Tolethorpe on the 11 May 1541, leaving the twenty-six year-old Anthony as his heir. Anthony was married to Joan Cyssel and the third son of their seven children was Robert, born at Tolethorpe Hall some time between 1550 and 1553. There is no record of his baptism only the date of his receiving a BA degree at Corpus Christi College, Cambridge, in 1572. Working backwards from this date suggests that he matriculated (entered) the College in 1570 when he would have been between fifteen and twenty years old, hence the suggested date of 1550 for his birth, although it could have been as late as 1555.

The two dates are interesting because if Robert Browne was born in 1550, England would have been strongly Protestant. When Henry VIII died in 1547, his son, Edward VI, was only nine years old. He had been brought up a Protestant rather than a Catholic and he was under the control of his uncle, Edward Seymour, as Lord Protector. Under Edward VI, all of England's parish churches changed to a new Protestant English Prayer book written by Thomas Cranmer. The old services of the Latin Mass ceased, the veneration of the saints and the remembrance of the departed were swept away. Stone monuments of saints in churches lost their heads and faces, wall-paintings were whitewashed over and stained-glass windows which had any hint of medieval superstition were smashed. The young King

Edward grew up to be a fanatical Protestant, but by 1552, he was already sickly. His father, Henry VIII, had ensured that the order of succession was part of English law, first Edward, then Mary, Henry's oldest daughter, then Elizabeth. So when Edward died in 1553, the Catholic Princess Mary would become Queen.

The Protestant leaders under Edward VI desperately tried to stop this happening by persuading Edward to alter the succession in favour of a Protestant. Lady Jane Grey had a distant claim to the throne as the great grand-daughter of Henry VII and could be their Protestant puppet. Before he died Edward signed the new order of succession. He had only been on the throne for six years. Lady Jane Grey was proclaimed Queen. But it was a vain attempt to thwart the Catholics. The people rallied to Mary and she became Queen a few days after Edward's death. England passed into the hands of a fanatical Catholic. All the churches changed back to the Roman Catholic Mass and, in 1554, Mary married the most powerful Catholic in Europe, King Philip of Spain. If they had a living child, the Catholic succession to the Throne of England would be assured.

Mary desperately wanted that child but no child came. She became convinced that this was God's judgement on England for the Protestant heresy which had swept through the land. She was sure that this heresy must be burned away by holy fire, the fire of execution. Protestant leaders were arrested and put on trial for their faith. Three former Fellows of Cambridge Colleges, Archbishop Thomas Cranmer, and Bishops Hugh Latimer and Nicholas Ridley, were tried for heresy. They were burnt at the stake in Oxford. Many other Protestant leaders fled to Geneva or Zurich, centres of the Protestant faith in Europe, while many ordinary men and women were caught and chose to die in the fire rather than renounce their Protestant faith.

Stamford was not a major centre of Reformation Protestantism and it is probable that little had changed under Edward VI so that under Mary, the re-introduction of the Latin Mass caused little upset. There were no Protestant martyrs in Stamford. But when England, as Spain's ally, became involved in Philip's war with France, the French attacked and captured the port of Calais. England lost her last toe-hold on the Continent, so ending the centuries-old existence of the Staple of Calais. Mary was blamed for the loss and her response to the news was to say:

'*when I am dead and chested* (my body opened), *ye shall find Calais engraved on my heart'*.

Charles Dickens wrote that it was more likely that they would find the names of the '*three hundred people burned alive within the four years of my wicked reign, including sixty women and forty little children.....'*

4. Growing up at Tolethorpe

If Robert Browne was born in 1550, a peaceful corner of rural Rutland was probably a very good place to be in for his infancy and childhood, as religious conflict brought terror and death to many English families. When Mary died in 1558, he would have been eight, old enough to be interested in exploring the countryside around Tolethorpe and the valley of the River Gwash.

The source of the River Gwash is near Knossington in Leicestershire near the western side of Rutland. The river flows east through lots of countryside and villages such as, Tickencote, Casterton, Tolethorpe, Ryhall and Belmesthorpe. After it passes north of Stamford, it enters the River Welland. The river is only about twenty miles long. It is a picturesque river that many people fish and paddle in. Many species of birds, fish and mammals live in and alongside the river and near the banks of the Gwash there are woods and grass lands.
(by Zack S., Abigail C., Amelia L. Owen S. and Owen W.)

The Gwash valley is an ancient landscape. Just to the west of Tolethorpe are the villages of Little and Great Casterton, where the Romans built their camp almost two thousand years ago to rest on the long march north up Ermine Street from London to Lincoln and York. Many of the villages and towns of the area have Saxon names, Oakham and Empingham, Exton and Hambleton but about a thousand years ago, the Vikings in their longships swept onto the east coast of Saxon England and Danish settlers spread inland.

They came up the valley of the River Welland and must have found the mouth of the little River Gwash just east of the Saxon town of Stamford. The valley offered rich pasture, good fishing and space in which to settle and they left a chain of villages and farms along the valley floor, all with typical Viking names. Belmersthorpe and Tollthorpe (now spelt Tolethorpe), Ingthorpe and Tickencote, and then, after the river disappears into what is now the great reservoir of Rutland Water, Gunthorpe and Martinsthorpe into the upper reaches of the Gwash.

The River Gwash at Ryhall Bridge today

The Gwash looks insignificant as it runs under the bridge in Ryhall today but it still provides some of the best fishing for brown trout and grayling in the Midlands. At the time when Robert Browne was a boy, growing up beside the river in the 1550s and 1560s, he must have fished for trout and grayling in the Gwash, just as pupils at Ryhall School do today.

I love to fish in the Gwash. The main fish caught is the brown trout – I've caught them twenty-four times – but the rarest fish I've caught is the beautiful grayling which I've caught seven times. Once, my Dad caught fifty brown trout in a challenge. I tried to catch the biggest trout once and it pulled me into the river. It was extremely annoying. My Dad is an expert at catching grayling and I saw him catch a grayling which weighed 2.06 pounds. He let me hold it and it was as light as a feather. I loved the colour of it and the taste. In the 1550s they probably did not have good fishing rods and they probably caught fish in the hand by 'tickling' for them. They might have even have used the ancient technique of spear fishing.

(by Gabriel G and Owen O.)

There is a famous English book on fishing, Isaac Walton's 'The Compleat Angler'. It was printed in 1633, the year of Robert Browne's death. Walton has good advice to offer those who want to fish for grayling in little rivers like the Gwash:

'First note that he grows not to the bigness of a Trout; for the biggest of them do not usually exceed eighteen inches. He lives in such rivers as the Trout does; and is usually taken with the same baits as the Trout is, and after the same manner; for he will bite both at the minnow, or worm, or fly, though he bites not often at the minnow, and is very gamesome at the fly...He has been taken with a fly made of the red feathers of a paroquet, a strange outlandish bird; and he will rise at a fly not unlike a gnat, or a small moth, or, indeed, at most flies that are not too big. He is a fish that lurks close all winter, but is very pleasant and jolly after mid-April, and in May, and in the hot months. He is of a very fine shape, his flesh is white, his

teeth, those little ones that he has, are in his throat, yet he has so tender a mouth, that he is oftener lost after an angler has hooked him than any other fish.....'

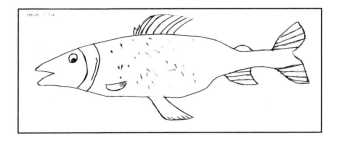

A grayling by Mitchell G.

In Robert Browne's time at Tolethorpe, it is even possible that the River Gwash had a run of salmon, coming up the River Welland from the sea as the Vikings had done. There is a hill at the west end of Rutland Water still called Lax Hill. As 'lax' is the Viking (Danish/Norwegian) name for salmon, could it be that here the hen salmon scraped hollows for her eggs in the gravel beds of the shallow waters of the Gwash to be fertilized by the cock salmon's milt to produce the next generation? If this was true, there would have been a bounty of tired salmon at the foot of Lax Hill, easy to catch for the kitchen at Gunthorpe Hall when fish was needed on Fridays.

This beautiful little valley, including the village of Little Casteron and the Tolethorpe Hall estate, is now preserved as a Conservation Area. The poet, John Clare (1793-1864), who was born not far away at Helpston, courted the love of his life on walks along the riverbank. He wrote of the peace and pleasure he experienced while sitting on the bank, in his poem, *The River Gwash*:

WHERE winding Gwash whirls round its wildest scene,
On this romantic bend I sit me down;..........................
Oh, thus while musing wild, I'm doubly blest,
My woes unheeding, and my heart at rest.

Amelia L. wrote her own acrostic poem about this lovely place:

Rushing merrily under curving bridges the river flows on,
In the murky depths of the Gwash lie tiny tiddlers hiding
* from their foes,*
Vivid flowers are made to bow down to the passing water by
* the strength of the wind,*
Eels slither slyly along the pebbly bottom amongst slimy
* weeds,*
Rustling trees whistle calmly in the soft breeze,

Gliding past the cream coloured sand and dewy banks the
* river meanders on,*
Waiting patiently for the fish to bite, children sit balancing
* on a fallen tree trunk,*
Azure blue water is being splashed all over the place by a
* swimming dog,*
Stinging nettles invade the spare space on the banks as all
* the other plants try to fight back,*
Happily the Gwash slides into the River Welland and all is
* calm...*

(by Amelia L.)

As a child, Robert Browne would have walked with the family across the meadows to the stone church of All Saints at Little Casterton. It too is a peaceful place and the path to worship is still there, through the flock of sheep and into the churchyard through a gate. The ancient church has medieval wall-paintings which have been partially white-washed over. Could this have happened in Robert's childhood when the Protestant reformers wanted to remove all images of saints from the walls of their churches? Set into the chancel floor is an inscribed slab memorial to Christopher Browne, his great-grandfather.

We know none of the details of Robert's early life at Tolethorpe. As the son of a well-off landowner, he was probably taught by a Tutor at home rather than face the rigours of an Elizabethan schoolroom. He would have 'learnt his letters' from a horn book until he could read and write. Once he had mastered the basics of reading and writing he would have learnt Latin, the common language of all educated men in Europe, and perhaps even a little Greek, with a tutor who may have been a former student at the University of Cambridge.

5. Becoming a Separatist

Cambridge at that time was a great centre of Protestant teaching where many of the leading scholars of the Reformation worked together. The Lady Margaret Professor of Theology in the University was Thomas Cartwright and his sermons in Great St Mary's Church were said to be so popular that they had to take the glass out of the church windows so that those outside could hear.

Thomas Cartwright was born in Hertfordshire in 1535 and studied at St John's College in Cambridge. He allowed himself only five hours sleep a night because he chose to work instead, studying the Bible. He became the Lady Margaret Professor in 1569.

Robert Browne met Robert Harrison while they were both studying in Cambridge and they both attended Thomas Cartwright's lectures. They agreed with Cartwright's teaching when he said that everyone should not just believe what they were told but read for themselves from the Bible. They should not have to go to the parish church every week to pray from a book but worship in their own way.

(by Rhianna P. and Chloe B.)

Thomas Cartwright by Chloe B.

Cartwright taught that the Church of England was only 'half-reformed'. He had studied the Book of Acts in the New Testament. He found that, although St Paul wrote about 'bishops' in his letters to the first churches, there is no mention of the role of 'bishops' in the Book of Acts, St Luke's account of the first Christian communities. These were led by 'elders', members of their own community, rather than by leaders imposed from outside. He found that the first Christians in the towns of the Roman Empire met together to worship led by those who knew most about what Jesus had taught and governed themselves as congregations of worshippers. Cartwright taught that the Church in England should be fully reformed to include a return to this Early Church model but this teaching made him many enemies in the Church of England, especially amongst the Bishops.

Soon after Queen Elizabeth came to the throne of England in 1558, she appointed two Cambridge scholars to key positions in her new government. Matthew Parker, the former Master of Corpus Christi College, became her Archbishop of Canterbury, and William Cecil, of St John's College, became her Secretary and Chief Adviser. Between them, they worked out a new religious settlement in which England would be Protestant, but not extremely so.

After all the years of religious turmoil, Elizabeth and her advisers found a middle way which brought stability to her realm. Parliament was asked in 1559 to pass two Acts, firstly the Act of Supremacy in which Elizabeth was acknowledged as the Supreme Ruler of the Church of England and secondly, the Act of Uniformity, requiring all her subjects to attend worship in their local parish Church. The clergy were required to follow the services set out in the 1552 Prayer Book and the Church Wardens kept an eye on everyone in the village or town to check that they all came to church.

There is a record of a debate between Queen Elizabeth and some of the Bishops. When Elizabeth presented her ideas of religious reform to Parliament, the Bishops were outraged and began to argue

First Bishop: 'Madam, by this act, you force us to relinquish

our allegiance to the Holy Father.'
Elizabeth: 'How can I force you, Your Grace? I am a
woman.'
At this, the Bishops laughed.
Elizabeth: 'I have no desire to make windows into men's
souls. I simply ask, can any man, in truth, serve two
masters, and be faithful to both?'
The Bishops started to argue again.
Second Bishop: 'Madam, this is heresy!'
Elizabeth: 'No, Your Grace, this is common sense.'
The Bishops murmured in semi-agreement.
Elizabeth: 'Which is a most English virtue.'
At which, the Bishops laughed.

Outward conformity by attendance at church on Sundays was enough to show that her subjects were loyal members of the Church of England. If they wanted to remain Catholic and hear a private Mass or privately attend a sectarian meeting, that would be tolerated but they had to go to Church. Then, just at the time that Robert Browne was at Cambridge, the Pope in Rome issued a Bull, a formal statement which all Catholics had to accept as the truth. It described Elizabeth of England as a heretic and usurper of the throne. She was excommunicated from the Roman Catholic Church and all her Catholic English subjects were told that the Pope believed they had no allegiance to her. Even if they murdered her, they would be free from guilt in the eyes of the Roman Catholic Church. From this time on, all Catholics became potential traitors; they could not obey the Pope and serve the Queen.

There is a famous portrait of Queen Elizabeth on display in her childhood home, Hatfield House. It shows her holding a rainbow and wearing a magnificent gown. On the lapels of the gown, eyes and ears have been embroidered.

The message was clear. Wherever you live in England, Queen Elizabeth and her 'watchers' or secret police have their eye on you and you had better be careful what you say.

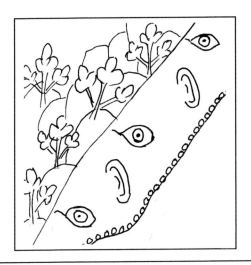

Detail of Queen Elizabeth's gown by Rhianna P.

Even amongst Protestants, not everyone was content with Elizabeth's middle way for the Church. Cartwright soon got into trouble. He was invited to debate the issues of authority in the Church with the Archbishop of York in front of Queen Elizabeth. He argued that the sovereignty of God did not need the support of kings and queens. Such views were very dangerous. When he continued to denounce the role of Bishops in the Church of England, Elizabeth and her advisers decided that he had to be silenced. He was sacked from his university post and driven into exile, first to Geneva and then to Holland. But his teaching influenced many at Cambridge and started a movement to fully reform, or 'purify' the Church of England from within. The leaders of this movement became known as 'Puritans'.

Some scholars wanted to go even further and leave the Church of England altogether, to *'separate themselves'*, from a church they thought could not or would not be 'purified'. They knew that St Paul had written to some early Christians advising them to have nothing to do with those with whom they disagreed.

'.....wherefore come out from among them, and be ye separate, saith the Lord,........'
(2 Corinthians 6 v. 17 in the King James Bible)

Some among the young men studying at Cambridge became the leaders of these 'Separatists', including John Penry from Peterhouse, John Greenwood from Corpus Christi College and Robert Browne also from Corpus.

Browne joined this Cambridge hotbed of religious controversy as an affluent young man from a privileged background. By the end of his first year, Cartwright had been deposed from his post as Professor but his teaching must have left an indelible impression on the young student. In 1572, the year that Browne completed his degree, thousands of French Protestants called Huguenots were murdered by Catholics in the St Bartholomew's Day Massacre. Many of the Huguenot survivors escaped as refugees to England. They settled in London and in Norwich where they joined other refugees from Catholic Europe.

Browne could have been ordained as a Minister in the Church of England when he left Cambridge. Many of his contemporaries were ordained but because he could not accept the role of Bishops in the church, he decided not to seek ordination. He is thought to have come back to Stamford to become a schoolmaster, possibly teaching at Stamford School. He is said to have been an effective teacher, keeping good order and earning the respect of the people of the town but he was restless and his views on the Church were radical. He wanted to share his growing conviction that the way the Church of England was governed was wrong.

When an outbreak of the plague in Stamford closed down the school, Browne went back to Cambridge and stayed from January 1578 with the Minister of Dry Drayton Church just outside the town. His host, the Rev Richard Greenham, agreed with Thomas Cartwright's Puritan teaching, the church should be governed by Elders or Presbyters and not by Bishops appointed by the Queen. He allowed Browne to teach and preach in his church and in the villages around. This was actually illegal as all preachers had to have a licence from the Bishop, but Browne ignored this requirement and continued without a licence until June 1579.

Anxious that Robert would get into trouble, his brother, Philip, applied on Robert's behalf to the Archbishop for a licence. When this was granted, as Browne had the necessary degree from the University, he was given the licence documents but treated them with disdain, losing one part and burning the other. He claimed that he had no wish to be licensed! The congregation of St Bene't's in Cambridge, the church which was also used by the students of Corpus Christi College as their chapel, invited Browne to preach there. He did so, openly criticising the way in which preachers had to be called and licensed by the Bishop. The people liked his sermons and even raised the funds to pay him for preaching. But he became ill and, when told by the officer of the Archbishop not to preach any more in Cambridge, he left. Together with Robert Harrison, the young Cambridge graduate who shared his views on the Church, he went to Norwich.

In 1580, Harrison was appointed Master of the Great Hospital in Norwich, an almshouse similar to Browne's Hospital in Stamford, except that it included provision for 'poor scholars'. He invited Browne to share his lodgings. The city was still full of refugees, Dutch Anabaptists who had left Holland and French Huguenots, many of whom were skilled weavers. They earned their living by establishing a cloth industry in Norwich using the abundance of English wool. Worsted cloth was first produced at this time and named after a Norfolk village.

Browne and Harrison gathered together a congregation of worshippers who began to meet in the Blackfriars Hall. This had been a Friary chapel before the Reformation but was not actually a parish church as it was used by the City of Norwich for meetings. They taught their listeners the importance of godly living and of not sharing their worship with those who were in their eyes '*wicked*'. Browne's preaching against '*prayer-book services*' was often very rude about the way in which people had to worship.

'*People are bridled like horses*' and they had to do everything like '*obedient puppies!*' he said. '*Hear, read, answer, kneel, sit, stand, begin, break off*'...the whole service was '*broken and taken out of the Mass book.*' He claimed that '*dumb and idle ministers maintained a vain worship without knowledge or feeling.*'

Browne continued to preach in Norwich in this way and began to '*move about and disturb the whole diocese of Norwich*', until Bishop Freke decided to act. He knew that this troublesome young man was related to the great William Cecil, by then Lord Burghley, Elizabeth's Secretary and Lord Treasurer, and one of the most powerful men in England. Freke wrote to Burghley to tell him that he had received complaints about his '*kinsman*' Browne from '*many godly preachers*'. They had told the Bishop that Robert was '*delivering vane and contentious doctrines*' and '*seducing the vulgar sort of people in meetings of one hundred in private houses and conventicles*'.

Burghley tried to calm things down. Writing back to Freke, he assured the Bishop that his young relative was acting '*out of zeal rather than malice*' and suggested that Browne should be sent to London '*to be conferred*' with. In other words, Burghley and others would try to talk Browne out of this rash behaviour. But when Browne got back to Norwich after meeting with Burghley, he continued to cause trouble with his preaching of '*strange and dangerous doctrines*'. The Bishop appealed for Burghley's help again.

Leah K. and Rebecca W. think that Lord Burghley would then have written a very angry letter to his kinsman:

Burghley House, Stamford
To my dear kinsman Robert,

*You are in gigantic trouble young man! I am **exhausted**, having to bail you out of prison every time, you little rebel! If I have to pay lots of money, you are in trouble. You think I am joking but I am serious. Why can't you just behave like you used to?! Or is that too much to ask?! I helped you out because you're my relative but now this is ridiculous! If this prison says no they won't release you.....well you're stuck! This is the last time, I'm not throwing my weight around anymore! When you're out PLEASE stay out of trouble, you rebellious devil! Next time you're in prison I'm not letting you out, you might as well die in there!*
Your kinsman,   William Cecil, Lord Burghley

Burghley House near Stamford which William Cecil, Lord Burghley, kinsman to Robert Browne, started in 1555 and completed by 1587.

In spite of all Burghley's efforts, Browne was arrested again and imprisoned in London until the autumn of 1581. On his release, he and his followers in Norwich agreed that they could no longer stay in England.

'The Lord did call them out of England'.

Later that year they fled to Holland and joined an English community in the city of Middleburgh in the province of Zeeland in the extreme south of Holland. Thomas Cartwright and his followers had already settled in that city. Ben D. thinks that Robert will have written home to let his friends know of his escape:

Today I have just finished my journey to Holland! I am really glad because I have been travelling for about three and a half weeks. Now I have the problem of how am I going to be able to preach to my followers? It is simple. Books! That's right, books. I am confident that this will work

but I am worried about what may happen to my followers.
(by Ben D.)

While the Bishop of Norwich and Lord Burghley were struggling to control the troublesome Browne, the English parliament had passed Acts against Catholics. In 1580, the fine for not attending church services on Sundays was increased from twelve pence to twenty pounds with imprisonment for repeat offences. Converting to Catholicism or trying to convert an individual to Catholicism became an offence of treason, punishable by the terrible traitor's death of hanging, drawing and quartering.

As the Pope encouraged young English Catholics to train as priests in Rome and to return to England to support Catholics, Elizabeth's advisers, led by Sir Francis Walsingham, set up net-works of spies to catch them. If Catholic priests who were in England were caught, they were tortured, condemned as traitors and executed. *Rebekah W. and Leah K.* imagined what it would be like for a Catholic priest waiting in the Tower of London for his execution day and writing his last letter to his mother:

30th November 1581

Dear Mother

Tomorrow is my execution day. I am being held in the tower of London. The reason I'm here is because Queen Elizabeth found out I'm a Catholic priest. They say that they will hang me, take my guts out and cut me into quarters. I suppose that only a mother could love me. Please pray for me! I need it because the Queen is infuriated with me.
Your loving son,
Edmund Campion

While the English authorities were so busy keeping the country free from Catholic priests sent to undermine the

Government, the last thing they wanted was Protestants who would cause trouble by not conforming to the law requiring attendance at the services of the Church of England.

In Middleburgh, Robert Browne's little band of Separatist followers worshipped at first with Cartwright's group of English Puritans. But Browne and Cartwright fundamentally disagreed. Cartwright had always taught that the Church of England should be 'purified' from within. Browne's view, that it would be better to leave the Church of England altogether and become fully separated, could never be accepted by Cartwright. So at some stage the English Congregation in Middleburgh, already small, split in two. Browne and his followers set up on their own and he began to criticise his former teacher and even to write diatribes against him.

In a foreign land, with a shrinking group of supporters and unable to preach to English communities, Robert Browne turned to the only form of communication left to him. He began to write a series of pamphlets, trying to set out what he believed to be the future of the church.

6. 'Reformation without tarrying for anie'

Three of Browne's books were printed at Middleburgh in 1582, bound together to be sold as one volume and distributed to sympathisers. The pamphlets soon found their way back into England. The titles give an impression of the tone of his writing – confrontational, aggressive and rude:

'A Booke which sheweth the life and manners of all true Christians, and how unlike they are unto turkes and papists, and heathen folke....'

'A Treatise of Reformation without tarrying for Anie, and of the wickedness of those preachers, which will not reforme Themselves and their charge, because they will tarie till the Magistrate commande or compell them'

'A treatise upon the 23 of Matthew, both for an order of studying and handling the scriptures, and also avoiding the Popishe disorders, and ungodly communion of all false Christians, and especiallie of wicked preachers and hirelings'

Browne wrote as the classic 'angry young man' with scathing sarcasm about those who were so *'stuck fast in the myre and dirt of all Poperie that they cannot get out.....'*

He set out in the *'life and manners of all true Christians'* a blue-print for a new church, congregational in structure, to be led by its own elders who would only join with the elders of other similar churches to form a 'synod' for matters which affected them all. There would be no place for Bishops or licences to preach. Services would not have to

follow an approved 'prayer-book' and the church would not
be linked in any way to the authority of the state.

A Booke
WHICH SHEWETH THE
life *and manners of all true* Christians

And howe vnlike they are vnto Turkes and Papiftes
and Heathen folke.

Alfo the pointes and partes of all diui-
nitie, that is of the reuealed will and worde of God are
declared by their feuerall Definitions
and Diuifions in order as fol-
loweth.

¶ Alfo there goeth a Treatife before of
Reformation without tarying for anie, and of the wicked=
-neffe of thofe Preachers, which will not reforme them
felues and their charge, becaufe they will
tarie till the Magiftrate commaunde
and compell them.

By me, ROBERT BROWNE.
MIDDELBVRGH

¶ *Imprinted by Richarde Painter*
1582

The title page of the book by Robert Browne printed in
Middleburgh, Holland in 1582

48

Robert could not take these books back to England himself, but his followers could. The authorities in England were not long in responding to the appearance of these pamphlets on the streets of English cities. In 1583, a royal proclamation was issued which banned the selling of the books of Robert Browne and others and ordered the destruction of all copies of *'the same or suchlike seditious libels'*.

Robert still wanted more of his books to get back to England. So, he asked his companions to take them back with them in spite of the risks. When the companions got to England they started to sell Robert Browne's books. In the process, the Queen's officers saw them and arrested them. They were sent to prison and some were even executed for selling them. Robert Browne's most famous book was "Reformation without tarring for Anie." Robert Browne stayed in Holland for a few years then decided to go home.

(By Corey R. and Liam S.)

Elias Thacker and John Copping were two of those who were arrested for selling these books. They were caught in Bury St Edmunds, tried for sedition, convicted and executed by hanging. At their trial, they declared that they *'believed all things in those books to be good and godly'* and that they *'acknowledged Her Majesty chief ruler civil and no further'*. For their denial of Elizabeth as Head of the Church, they died. When it came to facing the law, ordinary men like Thacker and Copping were shown no mercy. Privileged men, with family links to the top, like Robert Browne, avoided extreme punishment. It was not just what you knew but who you knew that mattered.

In Middleburgh, as further disputes between the Separatist and the Puritan factions broke up the English church community, Robert Browne and his followers decided that they should leave. As England was hardly likely to welcome them, they chose to sail to Scotland, hoping to find a welcome among the Scots where there was no State church. They landed at Dundee and made their way to Edinburgh, preaching and distributing Browne's books.

He was soon in trouble again. The Presbyterian Church arrested him and his followers for causing a disturbance. Summoned to appear at the Kirk Session, the church court for hearing disputes, Browne was accused of criticising the Scottish Church for its lack of discipline. It seemed to Browne that it did not exclude those who were unworthy members. But when the Kirk Session met to hear his case, Browne refused to accept their authority, claiming to be subject only to the civil magistrates. That suited the Kirk Session, who handed him over to the magistrates. They promptly imprisoned him along with his followers!

When they were released in July 1584, he and his wife somehow made their way south into England, although the risks of arrest must have been great. Alice was heavily pregnant and returned to Stamford, where their daughter, Joan, was born. She was baptised at All Saints Church without Robert's agreement as he was again in prison by the time of Joan's birth.

Amy N. has imagined a letter written by Alice to her sister about the increasing strain of being married to Robert:

To my dearest sister,

Why did I ever marry this troublesome man? He is the biggest rebel around and puts on a huge mood every time I try and get him to come to church with us! People from all over know him as 'Trouble Church' which is awfully embarrassing for me, even though I love him very dearly. His friends all look up to him and are inspired by his inner strength. This is extremely annoying because they make a great fuss every time we go to church too. We have already had the Church Wardens at our door twice and next time Robert will have to go to prison again. We are going to have to think of ways to stop him going to a ghastly prison ever again.

Your loving sister,

Alice Browne

Browne himself was next heard of in London, where he was again preaching without a licence. He was arrested yet again by the Bishop of London and imprisoned. With these repeated times in prison, his health broke down and when Lord Burghley again intervened on his behalf, he was sent for examination by the Archbishop of Canterbury.

7. Conforming to the Bishops

Browne was, it seems, given a choice. He could either remain in prison, potentially for the rest of his life, separated from his wife and child, or he could sign a document to state that he accepted five statements:

1. to accept that he was subject to the Archbishop's authority under the Queen and not to resist or criticise it.
2. to accept that where the word of God was preached and the sacraments administered, there was the Church of God.
3. to accept that the Church of England was the Church of God and to promise that he would attend church according to Law.
4. to behave himself and keep the peace of the church, not preach or exercise the ministry of the church unless lawfully called to do so.
5. to participate in the Sacraments, including the baptism of his children yet unborn, and to encourage his servants to do likewise

Robert Browne signed on October 7th 1585. It was a humiliating climb down for the leader of the Separatists and he must have known that he would lose the respect of his followers for ever. He was released from prison, initially into his father's custody at Tolethorpe Hall.

After four months, Anthony Browne found the task of supervising his son too irksome and arranged with Lord Burghley for Robert to be held in Stamford under Burghley's supervision. This arrangement also broke down when Robert was found to be preaching in Northampton. He was summoned to appear before the Bishop of Peterborough, an appointment which he apparently failed, at first, to keep.

When the Bishop did interview Browne, it appears that he advised him to give up his ambitions of leadership in the church and to go back to his old profession of teaching.

In November 1586, Browne obtained the post of schoolmaster at St Olave's Grammar School, Southwark. The school Governors required him to sign an undertaking of good behaviour before they would allow him to take up this post. He agreed that he would not disturb the ministry of the parish and not attend any *'conventicles'* (illegal religious meetings) or confer with any *'suspected or disorderly persons'*. He agreed to bring his pupils to sermons in the church, to renounce any error he was found to hold and only use the authorised Catechism in the school. The Governors wanted to make sure that this former Separatist could not slip back into his old ways. If he was to be allowed to earn his living and support his wife and children, it could only be under strict terms.

For a time, Browne taught quietly at St Olave's following the terms of his contract. But it was not to last. He moved to another parish where he was less well known and began to miss church services. He quietly attended meetings which the church authorities would certainly have regarded as *'conventicles'* had they known about them. He began to write again, although his writing was not printed but circulated in private.

By 1587, Lord Burghley and Sir Francis Walsingham were busy tracking down Catholic plotters against the life of the Queen. They found clear evidence that implicated the Catholic Mary Queen of Scots in these plots. Although she was held in prison in England, her supporters had smuggled messages to her warning of a coming uprising against Elizabeth. She had become implicated in these plans. Mary was tried and convicted of plotting the death of the Queen.

Elizabeth hated the idea of having another Queen beheaded but she was eventually persuaded that she had no choice but to sign the death warrant. Mary was executed in Fotheringay Castle but England was still under threat.

Philip of Spain had also decided to end Elizabeth's reign by invading England with his armies from the Low Countries, but first he had to control the English Channel. A great Armada of ships set out from Spain on this 'Enterprise of England' but gales in the Channel and the skills of the English sea-captains defeated the Spanish. They were forced to sail for home right round the rocky coast of Scotland where many of them were ship-wrecked. Elizabeth was victorious and the church bells rang all over England.

Robert Browne was teaching in Southwark throughout these turbulent years, but his time at St Olave's Grammar School had come to an end by the autumn of 1591. He resigned his Mastership and again sought the help of Lord Burghley. Burghley sent him to the Bishop of Peterborough with a letter requesting that the Bishop '*look kindly on him and offer him ecclesiastical preferment*'. What they had in mind was that Browne, the leader of the Separatists and the 'Troubler' of the Church of England, should actually become a Church of England clergyman himself! It would clearly not be possible for the former leader of the Separatists to become a Church of England clergyman in London where he was well known and there were many Separatist '*conventicles*' still hanging on to a precarious survival. But it might be possible for Browne to become a clergyman in a quiet country parish in the Diocese of Peterborough.

Eve S. and Lucy H. think that he would have written to the Bishop:

My Lord Bishop,

As you know I come from a good family that made money by selling wool. I have been educated at Cambridge University at Corpus Christi College where I studied Theology. My first job was preaching at a church in Cambridge. A Vicar is my dream job and I would do anything to get it. I now need to provide for my family and hopefully you will consider my interest in being a vicar.

I am your humble servant,

R. Browne BA

Although only at the most just over forty, Browne was said by those most critical of him to be *'sound but his brain is sick'*. Always argumentative by nature, he was slowly showing signs of becoming more irritable and quarrelsome. It would be better if he could be found somewhere to live out his remaining years with the wife and children who remained loyal to him.

The Bishop agreed with Burghley's suggestion and Robert Browne was ordained into the Church of England clergy. His first church was very near to home, the parish church of All Saints in the village of Little Casterton, the church which his brother, Francis, attended with his family and to which all the servants from Tolethorpe Hall would have been taken, Sunday by Sunday. If a church in London had been deemed unsuitable, this arrangement of placing the troublesome Robert Browne right next to his former family home was clearly a mistake and he was only Vicar of Little Casterton for a few months in 1591.

The Parish Church of St John the Baptist at Achurch, Northamptonshire by Kieran L.

Lord Burghley found a much more suitable place in which to hide the troublesome Browne, a small village in the valley of the Nene not far from the town of Oundle. The post of Rector of the parish of Achurch-cum-Thorpe Waterville was vacant and, as Burghley was the patron, it was in his gift. The people of Little Casterton and Francis Browne must have heaved a sigh of relief as 'Parson Browne' and his wife and family were removed to the Nene valley.

Two years later, Queen Elizabeth's officers moved against Browne's successors as leaders of the Separatist Movement. John Pendry was arrested and accused of being the author of the Marlprelate Tracts, a series of pamphlets criticising the Archbishop of Canterbury in very scurrilous terms. Pendry was convicted under the Act of Uniformity and executed. Henry Barrow and John Greenwood, who led a Separatist church which met in Southwark, were arrested and imprisoned. They were convicted of sedition and hung in 1593. Before they died, all three of these leaders of the Separatist church must have been appalled at what they saw as Robert Browne's betrayal of the cause for which he had been imprisoned so many times and for which they were prepared to give their lives.

In 1603, Queen Elizabeth I died and the Scottish King, James I, came to the throne of England. He continued with the policies of the Elizabethan church although he did commission a new translation of the Bible. This was printed in 1611 and has become known as the King James, or Authorised, Bible.

King James VI of Scotland and I of England by Rhianna P.

8. Old age and a sad end

When the Rev Robert Browne became the Rector of Achurch in 1591, the hospital which his ancestor William Browne had founded in Stamford over a hundred years before was still looking after ten old men and two old women. Browne's Hospital is still there on Broad Street, although there have been some alterations to the original arrangements. The accommodation for the men in the large common room divided into ten spaces, each with its own window, was replaced in the Victorian period by a courtyard at the back surrounded by small cottages each for one resident. These were updated again in 1963 to flats each with a living room, bedroom, kitchen and bathroom. Today, the Hospital is still home to twelve residents in the care of the charity called the Foundation, eleven ladies and one man.

In Ryhall village there are two places for the elderly to live, the sheltered bungalows on one side of the road into the village and Frances Court Residential Home run by Spire Homes on the right. Ryhall residents who are retired and finding it difficult to look after themselves are well provided for.

Robert Browne continued to live independently and to continue in his role as a Rector well into his old age. Even if he had wanted a place at Browne's Hospital in Stamford, it was very unlikely that the Governors would have accepted him. A man notorious for being quarrelsome and argumentative would not have fitted easily into a residential community, no matter how tolerant the other residents tried to be. When he moved to Achurch-cum-Thorpe Waterville, he was only forty one at the most and hardly 'elderly'.

The pretty medieval parish church of St John the Baptist overlooks the meadows running down to the River

Nene and is well worth visiting, but there is little trace of the Rev Robert Browne. A paragraph in the information board does refer to his removal to Northampton in 1633, but the general impression is that Achurch would rather forget its association with such a controversial parson.

Even when Browne was alive and serving as Rector, there were those who recorded their critical comments about his behaviour. He was said to be a *'profaner of the Sabbath'* perhaps because he was a good musician and loved to play the lute while his eldest son, Timothy, played the bass viol in church on Sundays. Such music was frowned on by the good Puritan people of Achurch!

Another parishioner accused the parson of being a *'common beater of his poor wife whom he described as 'a cursed old woman'*. Alice Browne bore him seven children before she died in 1610 and cannot have been more than fifty five at her death. In 1618, Robert married his second wife in Stamford, but she died and was buried in Stamford in 1624. If they ever lived together, it seems that this was not in Achurch.

This is perhaps the origin of the comment by Thomas Fuller who lived just across the Nene in the village of Aldwinkle, that *'in my time, he (Browne) had a wife with whom he never lived, and a church in which he never preached'*. There is certainly no record of Robert Browne ever preaching in the parish church of St John the Baptist at Achurch.. His income from the Rectorship at Achurch was enough to provide for his family and for him to employ a succession of young curates to carry out most of his church duties, except for one. The Achurch parish register has over five hundred entries of baptisms, marriages and burials between 1591 and 1631, all in Browne's clear handwriting and with his signature, except for a ten year gap between 1617 and 1626.

Some of the entries include odd comments, such as the entries for the burials of Marie Hobson in July 1604, to which Browne has added *'an ould-poore maied'*, and for November 7th 1629, *'a childe of my own gracious Godsonne Robert Green baptized elsewhere in schisme'*.

So if he was not living in the Rectory and not preaching in the church, what was Robert Browne, Parson of Achurch, doing for all those years and what happened between 1617 and 1626? It seems that Browne had built a cottage in the neighbouring village of Thorpe Waterville within the same parish as Achurch and had lived there for most of his time in the area. Alongside his cottage he built a large room, which was called 'the old chapel', in which a group of worshippers met for services, rather than attending the parish church less than a mile away in Achurch. Robert Browne's real ministry seems to have been to the little Thorpe Waterville group who met in his house. They were effectively *'separatists'* although they attended worship led by their own Rector!

If this was the truth about Browne's ministry in Achurch and Thorpe Waterville, he appears to have got away with it from 1591 to 1616, when he was summoned to appear before the Bishop of Peterborough to explain his actions. When Browne failed to appear, the Bishop excommunicated him, depriving him of his post. The two curates maintained the register of Achurch Parish Church as well as running the church services until 1626. At some point, Browne met again with the Bishop and was re-admitted to the church so that he could take up again at least some of his duties.

Charles I became King of England in 1625 when Robert Browne would have been about seventy five. A man who had been argumentative from his twenties and had begun to show signs of mental disorder in his forties must have been well into senile dementia by then. His signature appears again in the register in 1626 and his entries continue up to 1631, by which year, Browne would probably have been over eighty years old.

King Charles I by Rhianna P.

Robert Browne was getting a lot older and starting to get grumpy. He was living in his house with his wife but not paying his taxes and the village Constable was keeping a record of this. In the end he needed to go and knock on Robert's door. When Robert answered the door he was shocked and surprised to see the constable. Then he realised what the constable had came for and anger bubbled up inside him. In fact, he was so angry he ended up punching the constable on the nose. Robert had to go to prison. He was old and surprisingly wide so when he tried to get on a horse, he simply fell off. So the constable went and got a cart, put a feather mattress on it and popped Robert on the mattress. He probably fell asleep on the mattress. When he woke up he was in prison in Northampton.

(by Amy N.)

The record shows that the Constable who took Browne before the local Magistrate, Sir Rowland St John, was actually his own godson, Richard Green. St John was inclined to pity the old man but assaulting a constable was a serious offence and Browne himself was so stubborn he seemed almost to want to go to prison. It would be by his own reckoning the thirty third time he had seen the inside of a gaol.

Browne got to Northampton Prison safely but he did not last long. In the record of burials of the nearby St Giles Church, the entry for the 8th October 1633 states that

'Mr Browne, Parson of Achurch, was buried.'

So the man who had William Browne of Stamford, the founder of Browne's Hospital in that town, as an ancestor ended his days in disgrace in the discomfort of Northampton Prison. He had lived during the reigns of Edward VI, Mary I, Elizabeth I, James I and Charles I. Four of them had claimed to be Head of the Church of England, a claim which Browne first denied and then had to accept, at least in public. But he retained to his end a reluctance to fully accept it, struggling to admit that the term 'church' could apply to parishioners who were forced to attend worship or to the ecclesiastical department of the state. In a bad pun, he claimed that

'There was no Established Church in the kingdom but his, and that was A-church'.

If Robert Browne left little trace in Achurch and less at Tolethorpe, how is he remembered? There is no grave stone in Northampton and no memorial to him at Achurch. We think that there should be some sort of memorial and Abbie H. has drawn a suitable gravestone:

His great-great-great-great-uncle William Browne left All Saints Church and William Browne's Hospital – stone monuments to his riches and his generosity. Robert Browne was never rich in money but he was rich in ideas and his real memorial is the survival of his ideas. His teaching that men should be free to worship as they wished and that the Church consists of a group of Christian people, not a building, have influenced Christian thinkers ever since. His refusal as a young man to accept that the Queen or King should have authority over the Church of England was not accepted at the time, but the whole issue of whether the Church of England should be 'established' as the State Church and whether Bishops should have authority and a special place in the Houses of Parliament are still debated vigorously today.

Since Browne's time, many 'free' churches, including the Baptists and the Methodists have been accepted in England, in the United States of America and all over the world. The Congregational Church looks back to Robert Browne as their founding father.

During his lifetime, his Separatist followers were called *'Brownists'* and groups of them continued to worship together illegally during the last years of Elizabeth's reign and into the time of James I. They were imprisoned for failing to attend their parish church services and some were executed for their refusal to accept the authority of the Queen over the church. But both Barrow and Greenwood refused to accept the name *'Brownist'* at their trial, believing that Robert Browne had betrayed their cause as indeed he had.

Their followers were called *'Barrowists'* but the name did not stick. When William Shakespeare wrote Twelfth Night, a play to be performed before Queen

Elizabeth towards the end of her long reign, he put into the mouth of Sir Andrew Aguecheek the line:

'for policy I hate; I had as lief be a Brownist as a politician'.

In other words, *'Brownists'* were a despised part of the community almost as bad as politicians!

They were still called *'Brownists'* when a group of Separatists meeting in the Nottinghamshire village of Scrooby decided to leave England and escape to Holland in 1607, just as Robert Browne and his followers had done twenty six years earlier. After a time in the Dutch city of Leyden, this 'Scrooby Separatist' group decided to cross the Atlantic in their ship the Mayflower and settled at Plymouth, Massachusetts. Ever since 1620, these Brownists have been known as the Pilgrim Fathers. Many believe them to be the founders of the United States of America, a company of faithful believers who were prepared to risk their lives and the lives of their children for the freedom to worship as they wished and not as they were told.

They, and the worshipping communities of the Congregational Churches across the world, are the real monument to Robert 'Troublechurch' Browne of Tolethorpe.

9. American Brownes/Browns

There were no Brownes or Browns amongst the Pilgrim Fathers original group from Scrooby. They reached Southampton from Holland but found that their ship, the Speedwell, was un-seaworthy. They had to combine with a group of 'planters', colonists with non-religious reasons for going to America, and sail with them in the Mayflower. Amongst the 'planters' there was a Peter Browne, although he had no links with the Separatists. He was a single man, a weaver by trade from Dorking in Surrey. When they reached New England, he settled with the rest in Plymouth Plantation. Many died in their first hard winter there and amongst the surviving women was a widow, Martha Ford. She and Peter Browne married and had two daughters, both of whom had large families, the older, Mary, had nine children, and the younger, Priscilla, had eight. But none of these took the name of Browne into the next generation and the Brownes of Plymouth Plantation died out when Peter died in 1633, the year of Robert Browne's death.

It appears that the first Browne owner of Tolethorpe Hall, Christopher, had a strong connection with Suffolk and had built a fine early Tudor house there. Swan Hall has survived and still stands just outside the pretty Suffolk village of Hawkedon, north-west of Sudbury. Christopher Browne must have built it before he bought Tolethorpe Hall in 1503. He died at Swan Hall in 1516. Two of his grandsons were born at Swan Hall and baptised at Hawkedon, Abraham Browne and Richard Browne. They both sailed from England for New England with the Winthrop Fleet in the Great Migration of 1630.

In the early 17th century, the Puritan movement in England had come under increasing pressure from the leaders of the Church to conform to the requirements of the Prayer Book. John Winthrop, a Suffolk lawyer, and a group of Lincolnshire Puritans linked to the Earl of Lincoln's family at Tattershall petitioned King Charles I for a charter for a new colony to be called the Massachusetts Bay Colony. It was to be Winthrop's *'city built on a hill'*, a Puritan community which would be a model for all future settlements. They left England in a great fleet of eleven ships carrying seven hundred passengers, many from the villages of Suffolk, landed first at Salem and went on to found the City of Boston, Massachusetts.

To the west of Boston, up the Charles River, Sir Richard Saltonstall, one of the Puritan leaders, established a new settlement at Watertown. Abraham and Richard Browne settled in this small community. Abraham was a surveyor and helped to lay out the plots and streets of the new town. His son, Abraham, built a house there, but when it was burnt down it was rebuilt by Abraham Browne's grandson, also Abraham. This house is still preserved as 'the Browne House', one of the oldest dwellings in North America.

Richard Browne became a Ruling Elder of the Watertown Church and when Governor Winthrop tried to impose a tax on all settlers in Massachusetts to finance the building of fortifications in Cambridge, Richard and the Watertown Minister led a protest against the tax. This was the first time that the principle of 'no taxation without representation' was expressed, which later became a theme of the Colony's opposition to the imposition of British taxes and the start of the War of Independence.

Between 1630 and 1640, thousands left England in the 'Great Migration', sometimes in whole communities led by their Puritan Ministers. Amongst them, on 'the Lion' in 1632, was another Browne family, John Browne, nephew of Abraham. He and his wife Dorothy, with their two young children, Mary and John, settled at Watertown, although they moved after a few years to Plymouth. By the end of the Seventeenth Century, the Brownes in the Thirteen Colonies of Colonial America had dropped the 'e' and spread far and wide.

According to some authorities on the Brown family in America, members of the family in Lexington, Massachusetts, had a part in the rising against the British which started the Revolutionary War, known to the British as the American War of Independence. Solomon Brown of Lexington is said to have fired the first shot that drew British blood on the Lexington Green in the skirmish starting that war and his first cousin, John Brown of Lexington, was one of the six "Minute Men" killed on the Green by the British on the morning of April 19, 1775. His name appears there on the war's first monument. Solomon's brother, artillery officer, Captain Oliver Brown, led the pulling down of the equestrian statue of George III the next year in New York City.

But as far as is known, there is no direct link between the Brownes of Stamford, England, and the most famous of all American Browns, John Brown, whose body *'lay a-mouldering in the grave'* according to the song:

> *John Brown's body lies a-mouldering in the grave,*
> *John Brown's body lies a-mouldering in the grave,*
> *But his soul goes marching on.*
>
> *Chorus: Glory, glory, hallelujah,*
> *Glory, glory, hallelujah,*
> *His soul goes marching on.*

He's gone to be a soldier in the Army of the Lord,
He's gone to be a soldier in the Army of the Lord,
His soul goes marching on.
Chorus: etc

During the American Civil War between the slave-owning states of the South and the Northern Union, this John Brown led an attack on Harpers Ferry on the Potomac River in Virginia. His plan was to capture a large arsenal of weapons with which he was going to arm slaves to fight the South, but the attack failed. Most of his raiding party were killed; Brown was wounded and captured and put on trial. He was hung as a traitor to the South, but to the North, he was a hero and the Northern Armies celebrated his memory in their marching song, *'John Brown's body'*.

This song became even more well known when Julia Ward Howe heard soldiers singing it and wrote her new words *'Mine eyes have seen the glory of the coming of the Lord;'*. This is now called the Battle Hymn of the Republic:

Mine eyes have seen the glory of the coming of the Lord:
He is trampling out the vintage where the grapes of wrath are stored;
He hath loosed the fateful lightning of His terrible swift sword:
His truth is marching on.
    Glory, glory, hallelujah!
    Glory, glory, hallelujah!
    Glory, glory, hallelujah!
    His truth is marching on.
I have seen Him in the watch-fires of a hundred circling camps,
They have builded Him an altar in the evening dews and damps;

I can read His righteous sentence by the dim and
flaring lamps:
His truth is marching on.
(Chorus)

This version, without the more military verses, has even found its way into many English hymn books which we use today.

In New England, Plymouth Plantation, and later Colony, continued to exist as a separate community under their own Governor until 1692 when it was absorbed into the Massachusetts Bay Colony and then into the State of Massachusetts. The Puritans of New England had finally overwhelmed the 'Brownists' of the Scrooby Separatists.

Their denominational successors, the Presbyterian and Congregational Churches, still maintained separate places of worship, on both sides of the Atlantic. In 1972 in England, the Presbyterian and Congregational Churches agreed to combine to form the United Reformed Church and the Congregational Church in Stamford became a United Reformed Church. But about six hundred English Congregational Churches decided not to join the new organisation. In Oakham and in many other East Midlands towns, the members of the Congregational Church still worship as a distinct denomination.

The spirit of freedom to worship as you wish is still alive and strong in the home area of Robert 'Troublechurch' Browne!

10. Brownes in Stamford today

We wondered what happened to the Browne family of Tolethorpe. The estate was owned by the Brownes up to 1751, when it passed into the ownership of the Trollope-Brownes. In 1864, it was bought by a banker, Charles Easton, who carried out major changes to the building, giving it the appearance it has today. Eaton became a Catholic and gave land in Stamford for the building of a Catholic Church, re-introducing to the town the first Catholic place of worship since the Reformation at the time of Robert Browne's birth.

The Tolethorpe estate was broken up and sold off in separate lots, ending up in the 1970s in a near derelict state. In 1977, the Hall and its grounds were bought by the Stamford Shakespeare Company to be developed as the home of the very successful Rutland Open Air Theatre. Every summer since 1977, the Stamford Shakespeare Company have staged three plays at Tolethorpe attracting audiences of thousands to this beautiful corner of rural England.

Since 2001, Tolethorpe Youth Drama has provided professional yet affordable tuition in drama for local young people from eight to eighteen. Their workshop based courses are unique in being at the heart of a working theatre and are based for the winter months in the historic surroundings of Tolethorpe Hall.

Brown is still a common family name, especially in Scotland, with former Prime-minister Gordon Brown a good example. But are there still Browns in Stamford and South Lincolnshire and do any of them spell their name 'Browne'?

To find out, Amy N. consulted the 'phone book for the area.

Many people living in South Lincolnshire today still go by the name Brown but without an E. In Stamford, twenty five Browns are listed in the 'phone book, spelling their name without an E. But there are about 2% (which is 3 people in Stamford) with an E on the end of Brown and there is one Solicitor in Stamford who has the surname Browne with an E on the end.

Places in Stamford built by William Browne are still standing today. These include All Saints Church and Browne's Hospital. You can still go and visit these buildings today, as they are very interesting.

(by Amy N.)

Chronology of the Browne family

1347 – English take Calais and set up 'Staple of Calais' to control wool trade

c1410 – William Browne of Stamford born

1442 – William and John Browne rebuild All Saints Church

1475 – building of William Browne's Hospital starts

1485 – Wars of the Roses end at the battle of Bosworth

1489 – William Browne and his wife Margaret both die

1492 – Columbus 'discovers' the New World

1503 – Christopher Browne, William's nephew, acquires Tolethorpe Hall

1509 – Henry VII dies and Henry VIII comes to the throne

1533 – Henry VIII marries Anne Boleyn

1536-1539 – dissolution of the Monasteries

1547 – Henry VIII dies and Edward VI comes to the throne

Between 1550 and 1556 – Robert Browne born, third son of Anthony Brown of Tolethorpe Hall

1553 – Edward VI dies; Lady Jane Grey queen for 9 days; Mary I becomes Queen; England reverts to Catholicism

1554 – Mary marries Philip II of Spain but Parliament refuses to have him crowned 'King of England'

1555 – Hooper, Bishop of Gloucester first to die as a Protestant; Archbishop Cranmer and Bishops Ridley and

Latimer burnt at Oxford; 300 Protestant burnt at the stake including many ordinary people

1557 - England loses Calais to the French

1558 – Mary dies and Elizabeth I becomes Queen - England reverts to Church of England with Elizabeth as Supreme Ruler of the Church - 1552 Book of Common Prayer re-introduced

1559 - Act of Supremacy and Act of Uniformity

1564 – William Shakespeare born

1570 - Pope issues a Bull excommunicating Elizabeth and absolving her subjects from allegiance and from guilt if they murdered her

1572 – Robert Browne awarded BA at Corpus Christi College, Cambridge

1572 – St Bartholomew's day massacre of Protestants in France – many Huguenots flee to England

1572-1575 Robert Browne taught school – possibly in Stamford or Southwark

1578 – returns to Tolethorpe and then moves to Cambridge

1579 – preaching in Cambridge – arrested, jailed, released
    (Robert Browne married Alice Allen from Yorkshire)

1580 – moved to Norwich with Robert Harrison

1580 – Religion Act: fines for failing to attend Parish church and imprisonment; illegal to attend a Mass, treason to convert to Catholicism or to attempt to convert anyone

1581 – Browne preaching in Bury St Edmunds – arrested

late 1581 – Browne and Harrison left for Middleburgh, Holland

1581 – Edmund Campion, Catholic priest, executed

1582 – Browne publishes three books in Middleburgh, Holland

1583 John Whitgift becomes Archbishop of Canterbury and begins suppression of Puritans in the Church of England including their writings – provoking the writing of the Marprelate tracts

1583 – June – Royal Proclamation commands destruction of all copies of Robert Browne's books; Elias Thacker and John Copping hanged in Bury St Edmunds for selling books

1583 – Separatist society in Middleburgh breaks up – Harrison and others join Cartwright's English Church – Browne and others sail for Scotland. – Browne writes an 'Answere to Master Cartright'

1584 – Browne summoned before Scottish Kirk Session – imprisoned – travels in Scotland

1584 July – Browne in London – preaching without a licence – publishes tracts – becomes ill – arrested and imprisoned – Burghley again intervenes and Browne committed to father's custody

1585 – at Tolethorpe but after 4 months, father no longer willing to be responsible for him - leaves to reside in Stamford under Burghley's supervision

!586 – Browne preaching in Northampton – cited to appear before Bishop of Peterborough – Brown refused to appear - excommunicated for contempt

1586 - Browne submits to authority of Bishops; appointed Master of St Olave's Grammar School, Southwark

1588 - crisis with Spain and the defeat of the Armada

1589 – Burghley sends Browne to Bishop of Peterborough

1591 – resigned Mastership of St Olave's GS – Browne becomes Rector of Achurch

1593 - Penry, Separatist, executed under Act of Uniformity - Barrow and Greenwood hung for sedition not heresy

1603 – March, Elizabeth I dies and James I becomes King

1605 – Gunpowder Plot fails

1607 – Jamestown, first English settlement in Americas is settled

1620 – Pilgrim Fathers settle in Plymouth, Massachusetts

1625 – James I dies and Charles I becomes King

1630 – Massachusetts Bay Company settles Boston

1631 June – last entry by Browne in Achurch Parish Register

1633 October – Robert Browne buried in Northampton

Sources

We used the following sources to research this book:

Browne, Robert *'A Treatise of Reformation ...'* 1582, Edition published for the Congregational Union 1903, T.G Crippen, reprinted as facsimile edition, Kessinger Publishing

Burrage, Champlin *'The true story of Robert Brown (1550?-1633) father of Congregationalism.....'* OUP 1906; reprinted as a facsimile edition, Bibliolife 2010

Harrison, Derek *'Tolethorpe Histories'* Stamford Shakespeare Company 2006

Hoskins, J. P., Newton P. A. and King D., *'The Hospital of William Browne, Merchant, Stamford, Lincolnshire; A History and an Account of the Buildings and Stained Glass'* printed by Peter Spiegl and Co, Stamford

Ireson A. S. *'The Stones of Stamford'* Stamford Development Committee 1986

Leaflet: *'The Hospital of William Browne'*, Stamford Civic Society

Rogers, Alan *'Noble Merchant - William Browne and Stamford in the 15th Century'* 2012 Abramis Academic Pubishing

Smith, Martin, *'Stamford Alsmshouses'* Stamford Vision 2015

Speed, John *'The Counties of Britain'* 1616, British Library edition, Pavilion Books 1995

Wright, J, *'History and Antiquities of Rutland'* 1684

and the following websites:

Elizabethan Puritanism - History

history.wisc.edu/sommerville/361/361-17.htm

Lilford Hall

www.lilfordhall.com/ElmesFamily/Robert-Browne.asp

Noncomformity in Norwich - HEART

www.heritagecity.org/research-cen...oncomformity-in-norwich.ht

Pilgrim Fathers - Lincs Reformed Church

www.lincs-reformed-church.com/pilgrims.html

Robert Browne Generally described as "the father of English ...

www.wecf-cong.org/articles/robertbrowne.pd

Tolethorpe Hall - Rutland Open Air Theatre

www.rutnet.co.uk/pp/gold/viewGold...3FIDType%3DPage%26ID%3D132

Thanks

Many individuals have helped with this book and we would like to thank them all:

At Ryhall Church of England Primary School

Mrs Sue Hallam, Headteacher, and Mr Ian Toon, Acting Headteacher; Ms Katia Watson, Class Teacher, and Mrs Sylvia Barrett, TA, of the Year 6 class, Mrs Clare Hicks, Class Teacher, and Mrs Julie Chapman, TA, of the Year 5 class; Mrs Diane Jibb, School Secretary; without the help of all of these, the book project would not have been possible.

The Pupils of Year 6 and Year 5, 2012/13

Additional help:

Mrs Molly Burkett and Mrs Jayne Thompson of Barny Books

Mr Hugo Spiegl of Spiegl Press Limited, Stamford

Mrs Joan Reeves for her expert proof reading

Mrs Jenny Haden of Oakham for her tolerance and support for the American Roots in English Soil (ARIES) Project